D1433357

How Elephants Lost their Wings

Retold by Lesley Sims

Designed and illustrated
by Katie Lovell

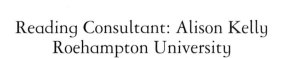

Reading Consultant: Alison Kelly
Roehampton University

This story is about flying elephants,

two gods,

houses,

peacocks

and
banana
trees.

3

Once upon a time,
elephants could fly.

They flew everywhere.

They flew high
into the sky...

and down to the ground.

They even
looped
the loop.

Sometimes, the gods flew on their backs.

But the elephants
were noisy.

They yelled, and
crowed like roosters.

Trees and houses
shook below them.

Cock-a-
doodle-
doo!

They flew into trees
and smashed them.

They landed on
houses...

and fell
right through.

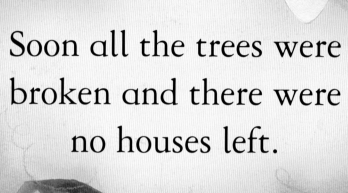

Soon all the trees were
broken and there were
no houses left.

"We must stop them,"
said the gods, and they
thought of a trick.

They invited the elephants to a grand feast. The elephants ate...

...and ate.

When their tummies
were full, they slept.

17

The gods took
away their wings.

They gave them to the peacocks

and the banana trees.

The elephants
were very cross.

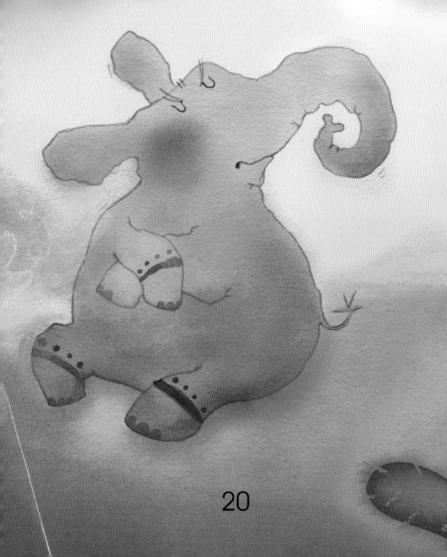

They shouted
and they stomped.

But they didn't get
their wings back

and they never
flew again.

Puzzles
Puzzle 1

Find these things
in the picture:

elephant
trunk
houses
hill
tree
wings

Puzzle 2

Can you spot the differences between these two pictures? There are six to find.

27

Puzzle 3

Put the pictures in order.

A

B

C

D

E

What happened next?

Puzzle 4

A

or

B?

Puzzle 5

A   or   **B?**

Answers to puzzles

Puzzle 1

wings

trunk

tree

houses

elephant

hill

Puzzle 2

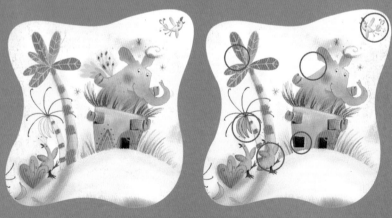

Puzzle 3

D  E  B

C  A

Puzzle 4

 → B

Puzzle 5

 → A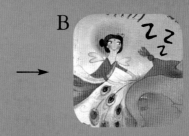

How Elephants lost their Wings is based on a folktale from India.

With thanks to Arshia Sattar
for advice on Indian mythology.
Digital manipulation: Nick Wakeford
Additional design: Caroline Spatz

First published in 2007 by Usborne Publishing Ltd., Usborne House,
83-85 Saffron Hill, London EC1N 8RT, England. www.usborne.com
Copyright © 2007 Usborne Publishing Ltd.